Pictures from the Bible 3

Emil Maier-F.

Jesus Befriends Zacchaeus

with a storytelling aid by Magdalena Spiegel

Abingdon Press
Nashville

ISBN 0-687-19958-1

Jesus Befriends Zacchaeus

Translation copyright © 1983 by Abingdon Press

All rights reserved.
Originally published as *Jesus macht Zachäus froh*

© 1980 Verlag Katholisches Bibelwerk GmbH, Stuttgart
under ISBN 3-460-24031-8

The scripture passages are from the Revised Standard Common Bible,
copyright © 1973 by the National Council of Churches of Christ, and are
used by permission.

Printed in Italy by A. Mondadori Verona

Jesus and his disciples were on their way to Jericho.

In this city lived Zacchaeus.

Zacchaeus was chief of the publicans, and he was very rich. He sat at the city gate and collected taxes for the Romans. He was allowed to keep some of this money for himself. But he kept too much. For this reason the people did not like Zacchaeus.

Jesus spoke to the people of Jericho. Zacchaeus also wanted to see Jesus. He was too short. He could not see over the crowd.

He ran to a fig tree.
Jesus had to pass by this tree.

The branches of the tree hung down.
Zacchaeus could climb up easily.

Jesus passed by the tree. He stopped. Jesus looked up and said, "Zacchaeus, come down quickly. Today I would like to have dinner at your house."

Happily Zacchaeus climbed down from the tree. He led Jesus and his disciples to his home.

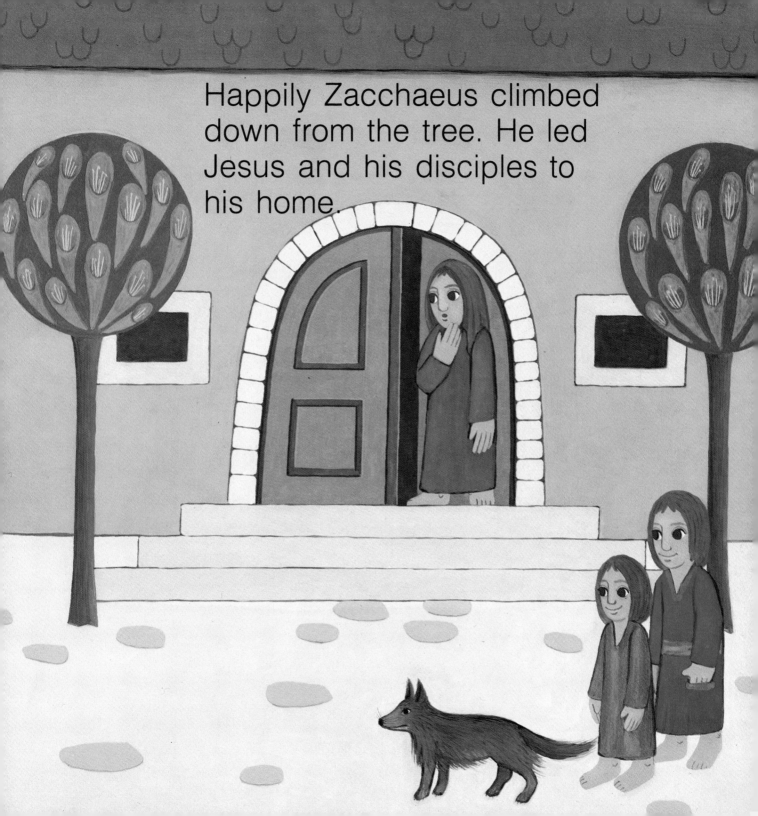

Before dinner Zacchaeus bathed the feet of Jesus.

Then they all sat down to eat. They had a real feast. Everyone was happy.
Happiest of all was Zacchaeus.

The people of Jericho, however, were shocked. "Jesus is visiting the man who cheats us when we pay taxes."

Jesus looked at Zacchaeus very lovingly. Zacchaeus was grateful and said, "Master, half of my money I want to give to the poor, and if I have taken too much from someone, I'll give him back four times as much."

Jesus said, "I have found you and made you happy. Today God's love has come into your house. You, Zacchaeus, are a child of God."

Zacchaeus kept his promise to Jesus.

For parents and educators in using this picture book

Before we look at this picture book with our children and tell them the Bible story, we should try to understand the contents and intentions of the book. This is essential. First we read the Bible passage to understand the whole concept of the message. Then let the words sink in, think about them, listen, let them "move in your heart." Only after we find the right approach to this message, can we present it to the children. We can then reach our goal, which is to persuade the children to have faith, love, and hope for present or future situations. Leading the children to the biblical happenings can be done two ways.

One is to tell the children the story first. This way we stay with the text and develop it to the better understanding of the child. By maintaining eye contact with the child, we can sense difficulty in understanding and can resolve it by repeating or expanding the text without adding a moralistic psychological meaning. The children listen to the story, their imagination and creativity will be stimulated, and they will picture the story. Only then should the pictures in the book be looked at, recognized, and the story related. Later the short text can be read, or the child may read the text for themselves.

A second possibility is to begin with the book. The pictures are shown as motivation. The children react spontaneously to it, express their feelings, which can be encouraged by parents or teachers. Let the children find out by themselves as much as possible.

Then the text of the picture book can be used and discussed. One can also freely explain without using the text. With both methods, the telling and looking at the pictures should not end the story. Discussions, drawings, playing different parts, singing, or a prayer can reinforce what the children heard and saw, and bring it closer to their own lives.

Jesus in the House of Zacchaeus
Luke 19:1-10

[1]He entered Jericho and was passing through. [2]And there was a man named Zacchaeus; he was a chief tax collector, and rich. [3]And he sought to see who Jesus was, but could not, on account of the crowd, because he was small of stature. [4]So he ran on ahead and climbed up into a sycamore tree to see him, for he was to pass that way. [5]And when Jesus came to the place, he looked up and said to him, "Zacchaeus, make haste and come down; for I must stay at your house today." [6]So he made haste and came down, and received him joyfully. [7]And when they saw it they all murmured, "He has gone in to be the guest of a man who is a sinner." [8]And Zacchaeus stood and said to the Lord, "Behold, Lord, the half of my goods I give to the poor; and if I have defrauded any one of anything, I restore it fourfold." [9] And Jesus said to him, "Today salvation has come to this house, since he also is a son of Abraham. [10]For the son of man came to seek and to save the lost."

Subject and Background of This Story

The New Testament Jericho was an important border city with a customhouse. The customs agents were civilians who had leased the right to collect taxes and duties for Rome. They had to turn over to the government a certain sum, which they in turn collected from the Jewish people. The chief customs agent was the chief of the customhouse, and the agents under him collected the money. With this system everyone worked greedily to fill his own pocket. Because of the rampant cheating, customs agents were hated by the Jews. They were not treated as part of the community and were compared with the sinners. Association with them was an annoyance and stirred up open hostilities.

When Jesus came into the city of Jericho, not one of the people made room for the chief customs agent. He, a small man, had no vantage point, he could not see Jesus. He had to climb up a tree to see. There Jesus saw him and called him by name. He went to his house and shared a meal with him. For the Jews that had a special significance. Sharing a meal was a sign of the kingdom of God, the future time of holiness. In Israel before dinner the feet of invited guests were bathed by the lowliest servant. The meeting with Jesus moved Zacchaeus spiritually. He was prepared to repent and to give back the ill-gotten goods. The restitution he promised went far beyond the expected. Jesus' answer quells those grumbling and pious ones who held against him the hospitality he had shown to a customs agent, an overt sinner. It puts his visit in perspective. He was friendly with Zacchaeus because he was a descendant of Abraham and belonged to Israel, the children of God. That was the mission of Jesus, the son of God, especially to go after the lost and castoffs and to lead them home into the kingdom of his father.

This story will impress children. It grants them multiple possibilities for identification. First, the children can readily identify with the small Zacchaeus, who could not see over the heads of others. Often children would like to be part of something, but adults won't give them a view. They form a wall. They won't let the children take part in something interesting, something that is important to them. Zacchaeus was not ashamed of his small size. He climbed up the tree where he could see Jesus. There Jesus saw him also.

Zacchaeus was not only short but also an outsider—one whom no one liked, who had no friends. However, Jesus saw Zacchaeus. He saw his need and loneliness. He gave him attention, the attention and consideration that his neighbors denied him! "I'm coming to your house!" "House" here means a great deal. "I'm coming to your house, within your four walls, into your family, not into your office." Jesus acted immediately without imposing preconditions or demanding explanations. He did not postpone his coming and did not console Zacchaeus because other things appeared more important to him. He said "Today I come."

And the others? The people of Jericho did not understand Jesus. "Why doesn't he come to our house? We are good and upstanding. We are certainly better than Zacchaeus, who took much more money from us than he should have. We have prepared ourselves for his visit, and now he doesn't come to us."

In order not to let this story slip into a cliché, it requires preparation and follow-through discussion and play. We should guide the children to be conscious of others and to be sensitive to what they are feeling. This skill can be developed, for example, through the study of photographs. The subject is not one of being pretty or ugly but rather the feelings of these persons. What does his facial expression say? What does he want to express with his gestures? If it deals with the problem of being an outsider, one must be very careful. A child will easily identify with this role.

Let's talk about the story. It instructs in discrete ways. We must try to follow the deeds of Jesus in our actions since he came especially for the lonely and castoff and wanted to make them happy. How often do we push people back or offend them! We should be open to outsiders, turn to them, look at them, sense what they feel, and bring them into our life. Whoever feels like an outsider should not stay in isolation, but should become involved, climb over the barriers, speak up, react. Then is change in life possible.